Preface

When I decided to write this book, I thought of it as a tool to help people get through bad times. The bad times I am referring to are times of financial distress in business…and what this does to the business, the relationships we have, and to the person. There is a great physical and mental drain on people as they face challenge.

This book is about my journey in small business and some of the life lessons that resulted. It is a result of conditions I experienced and lived through. The impact that experience left caused me to look at others going through crisis and figure out a way to reach out to them.

The purpose of this writing is to provide insights, support, and hope for "light at the end of the tunnel" for those who are trying so hard to find their way through the challenges of today's economy.

I am committed to helping others through the trauma and stress of conducting business in an uncertain climate in less than favorable economic conditions. I am also adamant about sharing avenues of action which lead to a positive result of restored calm, confidence, and a sense of personal and professional satisfaction.

My sincere good wishes to each reader for successful and peaceful resolve to your life's challenges.

Sharon Miller

Sharon Miller
President and Owner
ITH Staffing

About the Author...

Sharon Miller is a talented businesswoman who has enjoyed the success of multiple entrepreneurial ventures. Her efforts have earned local, state, and national recognition.

Despite her hard work, careful planning, and informed decision-making, the day came when she found herself in stress up to her ear lobes...looking for solutions to reduce the pain and help her save face, so she could get on with her life.

For this vivacious mother of two accomplished daughters and six talented grandchildren, she was determined to make her way through this deep economic and emotional valley and return to higher ground of resolve and peace.

In this writing, Sharon shares her feeling with gut-retching honesty and allows the reader to see behind the mask of perpetual success. Why expose herself? Because she is a winner who is dedicated to helping other business women and men move to the winners' circle with her.

Easing the pain others may experience by documenting her own journey stands as testimony that no person is alone...we can learn from each other...grow and survive together. I applaud her courage, strength and success.

Author Endorsement written by:

Dr. Judith Burton, Ph.D.
President, Burton & Associates

What You Will Learn from this Book…

1. Look for cost, time and results. Do your research. As you are selecting professionals to assist you, ask for hourly rates and ask for estimates on total charges. Find out what the timing will be on working through this situation. Get references and call the references. Ask the hard questions. Pin the professional down on what they anticipate the results to be.

2. Process. Find out what you need to do, what they will do for you and the process. What I found out is that a lot of information is requested and then there are vast time spans when it appears that nothing is happening. Request updates on progress on a regular basis. This update might be monthly, it might be quarterly. Get an outline of what is going to happen and who makes it happen.

3. Readiness to change. Get ready, because you can't do business in the future the way you've done it in the past. It didn't work. There needs to be an openness to change, to pass the responsibility of what you can't do well, or what you don't like to do on to someone who does it well. Sometimes that means they tell you no to ideas and you have to listen. It might mean you have to give up some of your ownership in the business to save the ship. If you are a person who needs to be in control, as I am, it will take a lot of self talk and discipline to admit your weakness, to admit you just don't want to do it all anymore.

4. Do you work in the business or own the business? Maybe you have to do both. Maybe you shouldn't do both. Each situation is different, it depends on the number of employees and outside services you have to work with. It is very difficult to be strategic and keep your eyes on the future, when you have to answer the phone and deal with details of the day-to-day business.

5. Understand your Profit and Loss Statement. If you don't understand it, take a class, go online, or get a friend. Ask lots of questions from your advisor, the CPA and the Attorney.

6. Learn enough about your accounting software so you can get into it and print reports.

7. Look at staff. Do you have the right people doing the right jobs? Do you have people who need to find a new job? These are the hard decisions to make. I had to ask myself if anyone ever stayed working for

me because they worried about what I would do when they left. The answer was no. That made any changes I had to make easier. I can also tell you that the people I let go (for the most part) are still friendly with me and are in a better match than they were when working for me.

8. Review all contracts you have. Telephone, IT support, photo copiers, postage machines, and the lists go on. Make sure you can put your hands on them, you will need them.

9. Protect your assets. This is where professionals come in. You must be legal, but there are ways to be wise and position yourself and your family to suffer as little as possible.

10. What do you share with your customers and the community? Do you continue on and act like nothing is wrong. Do you tell the world? These are questions that must be answered, but depends on who your customers are and what your business is.

11. Behavioral changes are a must, both to existing staff and, most important, to you. We missed the mark someplace. Often it is circumstances, but at some point we have to see the warning signs sooner to avoid future problems. We have to look at the business as a business, not a family, not a game-but a business.

12. How much information do we share with family and close friends? When do we tell our close family and what do we tell them? Do we say we are out of control? Do we say we are failures? We will explore the what and when of sharing throughout the book.

Real Life...

Adding to this cycle is:
- Depression
- Sleeplessness
- Headaches
- Low Self-Esteem
- Hopelessness
- Helplessness
- Lack of Energy
- Fear of Failure

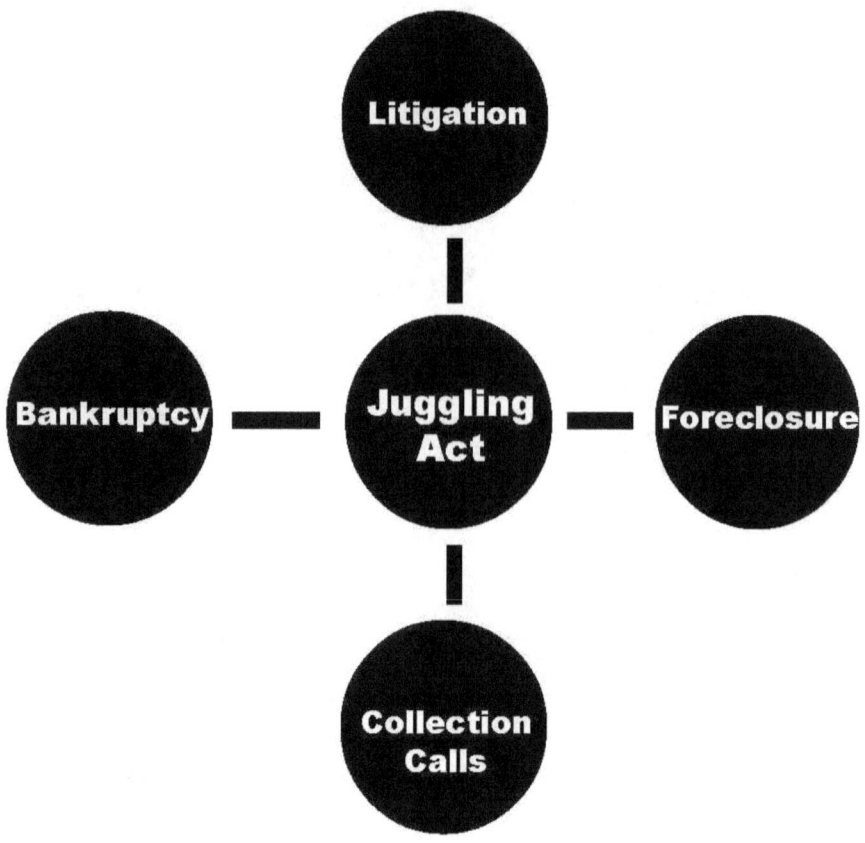

And there is more to juggle:
- Decline in Revenue
- Threatening Letters
- Documents
- Accounting Issues
- Reduced Workforce
- Increased Operating Expenses
- Reduced Cash Flow

In the Beginning…

People enter into business for a lot of reasons. Sometimes it just happens. You have a talent or skill and through sharing this with other people it becomes a business. Passion for a craft or cause will also be the root cause for business just happening.

Control over one's life is another reason many go into business for themselves. When people leave the corporate world and go into small business they feel they will have control. What they soon realize is you have traded one kind of control for another. You may be able to start your day at 10:00 a.m. rather than 8:00 a.m., but when a deadline nears you will work around the clock if that is what it takes. You might be able to write your own business plan, but you also have to fund that plan. You also have to take responsibility for all aspects of the business. The buck stops at your feet. In good times that control is a great thing. In bad times, that control often outweighs a person's coping ability.

Once you are in business there is a chance that problems can develop. There are many reasons this might happen. Lack of capital, the economy, lack of business knowledge, outside demands, illness, legal issues, bad debts, and surprise expenses are a few of the reasons problems develop. Reacting to these problems varies depending on the problems and the resources available.

There are many factors that cause businesses to fail but usually it isn't about the owner's commitment to the work or their lack of knowledge about their industry. A significant problem is the owner's commitment to the employees and a lack of knowledge regarding business practices and finance.

The root cause of business failure or crisis must be identified. Too many employees, too much overtime, too many family members on the payroll, and no knowledge of the cost of the goods or services being offered are just a few of the instances where a hiccup in normal operations causes a snowball effect that becomes an insurmountable problem.

Cash flow is another area that can cause a business to enter the "crisis" state. Businesses pay their bills on time, then they lose a major account, customers extend their credit terms, or a customer goes out of business leaving the employer with a bad debt . These can totally destroy the profitability of the business.

Most business owners are very proud people and view the business as a reflection of themselves. Hard work, countless hours and large sums of money have been invested. Business owners start dumping personal money into the business, making what was a corporate liability into a personal liability. IRA's and 401(k)'s are eroded. Their retirement is gone. This is one of the biggest mistakes business owners make. They lose their retirement and get hit with additional penalties and fees that just compound the problem. Personal money is used to keep the business afloat. Employees continue to get paid and keep their jobs because the business owner feels an obligation to them. It is easy to look at numbers and tell someone to fire employees. It is very difficult for a business owner to fire someone who depends on them for their livelihood. These employees are often part of the "family."

The right decision is very difficult when dealing with and feeling responsible for the livelihood of friends and family. When business owners hesitate with adjusting payroll, it often brings the house of cards down. The liabilities escalate; the business operates at a loss.

Business owners put personal money in their businesses so they don't have to fire anyone. We see people all the time who have worked for years and can't cash a paycheck because there isn't enough money, but they continue to pay employees (often employees who are not needed). As noble as that is, the only outcome realized will be the loss of jobs for employees and owner.

Every small business owner must look at their business and make a decision regarding the future. Sometimes closing the doors is the right answer. The important decision is when, and planning for the closure. Failing to make a decision often results in a decision being made for you. The make-up of a business owner usually includes the need for control. Controlling a closing is better than being shut down.

Small business owners can't get loans, so they pay payroll, insurances, rent, etc. and miss the payroll taxes. The intention is to pay it late, but interest and penalties occur and paying it back becomes impossible. This loan isn't really a loan. It is a theft. Small business owners do not think of it that way; however the money belongs to the IRS and half of it is from the employees' paychecks.

It takes awhile for the IRS to spot the problem but trust me, they will. When the IRS spots the problem, you will hear from them and it will not be pleasant. These debts escalate quickly and you just spiral downward. If left long enough, the IRS will close you down.

If you find yourself with business problems, seek help immediately. Help is available.

One day you look at the desk and the bills outnumber the income. The sales are down, expenses are up. Overhead stays the same. You question yourself, "What did I do wrong? Did I fail to act as soon as I should?" Emotion and the need for control take over. You get busy doing something, anything you can control. I emptied the wastebasket, cleaned drawers, and updated my contact lists. These were things I knew I could do and have an impact on. When I left the office I went to the kitchen and cooked. I cooked because people always told me how they enjoyed the dishes I prepared. I gave food away to anyone I could think of. Some people go to the gym, ride bikes, fish, sleep, eat, gamble, drink and become addicted to drugs. God walked with me and I resorted to cleaning and cooking.

Mindset of an entrepreneur...

People differ in many ways. There are the followers and the leaders. Leaders come in several forms. There is the leader who leads the army using someone else's rules. Managers in a union environment are an example of this kind of leader. Then there are those who create the rules and employ others to implement. I would call these people 2nd phase small and medium-sized business owners. They know what they want but are not interested in the day-to-day implementation. They are the visionaries.

The last group and the group that I fit into is the small business entrepreneur. Fiercely independent. Has a can do/must do attitude. I was raised in a family where work was worshipped and everything could be accomplished by hard work.

Over the past thirty years I have been counseled, gone through a reorganization of businesses, and shared my experiences with hundreds of others feeling the desperation of the experience. So hard work, or lack of it, was/is not the reason for difficulties and failure. I tell people all the time that the bankruptcy courts, attorneys, workout specialists and consultants were not created for one person. Historically speaking, there are business failures. When big business fails or runs into difficulty it is a bad situation, but big business doesn't have one or two owners. It isn't personal. In small business the failure is personal.

Small business owners take on the identity of their business so much so that there is no separation between personal health and success, and business health and success. So much so that small business owners are apt to put their own money into the business when the times get hard. Workers and stockholders of big business would never do this. Big business stockholders are not held personally liable for business problems either. Small business owners sign their personal assets as guarantees for financing. Society has helped create the personal/business persona the small business owner accepts.

When a small business owner gets in trouble, pride is the first obstacle. Then comes the responsibility to care for those that work for you. I have been in business for 35+ years and I have never had an employee who postponed leaving when they wanted to. No one has ever continued employment because they thought they were responsible for me. I have postponed releasing people because I felt responsible for them.

Entrepreneurs are usually very creative people and they want to come up with solutions. They are also wishful thinkers, so they feel that the fix is just ahead. Entrepreneurs hold on longer than they should. They have a need to be in control.

Personally, I used poor judgment on many fronts. I trusted employees to do the jobs they were hired to do. In some cases they didn't give me the information needed to deal with problems early on. In some cases they weren't qualified to do the job. They didn't know and neither did I. There are also outside influences such as lawsuits, recalculation of unemployment or worker's compensation expenses, loss of a large customer, a bad debt created by a larger customer, increases in interest, the economy and many more. Each person has his or her own reasons. It isn't one reason, it is many.

What happens is we avoid and deny the problems. We let them slide and then they begin to snowball. We start by paying things a little later, or not paying them at all. We work ourselves into a deeper hole. We don't ask for professional help soon enough. We don't know who to ask. We are afraid. We are embarrassed. We have family obligations.

We feel alone and we feel like no one has ever encountered situations like we are. We wish away the days and then lay sleepless all night worrying about the next day. If the individual drinks or has access to drugs, these can come into play at this time. We role play, we continue to go to meetings and family gatherings. We are physically there, usually with a smile on our face, but our mind is not there. We distance ourselves from others. We change our spending habits. We don't go to as many functions that have a price tag attached.

We become paralyzed. We look at the stacks of paperwork. We don't open some of the mail. We are afraid.

Recognize you need help,

If we are wise enough or lucky enough or get pushed into a corner we seek help. This help can be that of an attorney, a CPA, a turnaround specialist, a tax and business consultant. My advice is to get someone who specializes in helping troubled businesses get better or close the business. Don't continue to spiral downward.

The attorney and CPA do many things, but they do not specialize in troubled businesses. My advice is to get a qualified consultant and then work with them to identify the appropriate attorney, CPA, et al. This might include money sources, supply sources, investors, and other needed components to make the business turn around.

Also, just because someone is a CPA or an attorney doesn't mean they have all the right answers. Make sure you like and can work with the people you hire. Remember you are hiring them and you have to trust them. It is important to follow the advice of the right people. Sometimes someone with a turnaround management background, a workout specialty or a business consultant with experience dealing with the IRS and other taxing entities and lending sources is best.

We have to be willing to listen to the consultant. We have to know what we want. If the consultant says this business cannot be saved, are we ready to deal with that? If not, what are we going to do? This can cause health issues, emotional issues and relationship issues. Sometimes it causes suicide, often divorces and loss of friendships. We lose memberships in clubs, houses and credit card privileges. We get despondent.

When we talk with the consultant we give answers. Sometimes we don't understand the questions and so we don't give the complete answer. Sometimes we can't remember. (Is this God's way of saying enough is enough?) We get so exhausted we have memory lapses. We don't know what to pray for or what to plan for. It seems that the future holds nothing for us. We just float.

When going through financial problems, whether they are IRS, State/Local Taxes, Unemployment, Worker's Compensation, bills that you cannot pay, legal or accounting, they all look alike. It is a downward spiral. You pay a bill, but there are late charges or penalties and interest. If it is a utilities bill, it often requires a deposit to reinstate the service. The list goes on. Not everyone has the same evil spirits to deal with but we all have evil spirits of some kind.

Then there are liens and lawsuits. If you close a facility there is a lease to deal with. If you cannot pay the payments a lawsuit results and then you have additional attorney fees and personal time. With all problems come accounting and legal fees.

You pile the problems up. Sometimes you can't bear to open the envelope so you don't. That gets you in trouble because some issues are time sensitive.

Business people are risk takers by nature and sometimes we decide to take risks and try to go into a new venture to get us out of the hole. Some of the ventures only get us further into the hole. Be cautious.

I would advise anyone going through this problem to pick one person you know and trust and share with them what you are going through. Keep them informed of what is happening. Ask this person for grounding, encouragement and help when needed. Keep your confidants to a small group. You will get conflicting information if you don't.

My life experience...

I am an avid reader. I read for fun, I read for business, I read for spiritual guidance. I have read more books on how to and why than I could name as they relate to business. In my reading I usually get the feeling that the information is purely academic and not practical life experience.

Life experience carries emotion; academic does not. The personal side of what one goes through in troubled times must be different for each person, but I can speak for my inner feelings as I have encountered the hard times.

First we deal with pride. Business owners are risk takers by trait. They look to the future and are not always so good at dealing with today. Control people would be another description of this kind of person. How to react and respond to crisis beyond our control is a major wall that we encounter. Maybe there is a gender difference in this entire emotional issue. I have talked to many people over the years and I can tell you that everyone I have talked to who is experiencing business or personal challenges, reacts in one manner or another.

Thoughts and Feelings I experienced…

- I'm going to explode.

- I don't know what to do.

- I don't understand how the system works.

- What have I done to deserve being punished like this?

- Why me?

- Help!

- I am all alone.

- There is a tomorrow.

- Starting over.

- Retreat.

- Can't concentrate.

- Establish a plan.

- Listen to your heart and mind.

- Work with a professional you can communicate with and understand.

- How do I pay for the professional help?

- Where does future money come from?

- I'm too old to start over.

- The lawyers.

- The money.

- The accountants.

- The consultants.

- The creditors.

- The waiting.

- The details.

- The "gotcha" game.

- Family.

- Friends.

- Workers.

- The tainted feeling.

Real Life Stories…

I have a friend who I call the visionary. He is so busy looking at the future he doesn't have time or can't deal with the issues of the day. Many of the people who deal with this person think he has some kind of attention deficit disorder or he is, to quote them, "crazy". He isn't crazy. He is crazed. He has been successful. He has been at the top. He has now lost his home and his business. He is in debt, in bankruptcy, has an old (15 years) car and depends on Social Security to see him through. His wife is a mess. She is at the end of her coping ability. Five years ago this couple had a 2 million dollar home and successful business. The economy and some poor decisions put them where they are today. I admire my friend. He continues to keep moving. He will win the game based on the theory of numbers. He is willing to stick his neck out, willing to recruit people to finance his ideas. My friend is working as a self-proclaimed broker, putting ideas and people together. I have no doubt that eventually he will succeed. Will he ever be back to where he was five years ago? Probably not. Will he be happy? Absolutely. What he has is spirit. He doesn't have a large fan base at this time, but he does have vision and the self-confidence that he can do it. He also has a deep faith and a desire to make a difference. I share this story to give you a glimpse of how a 60-something year old male handles challenge.

I will share another story and then I will get back to my own emotion and how I tackle the problems. This story is about a 70-year-old African American woman who was also at the top of her game. She had a twenty million dollar business and had received many awards and recognitions for her work and community involvement in her Florida community. Over the course of three years her husband was sick and died. She stayed home with him for several months and ran the business from a distance. She lost a major contract with the State of Florida. The economy took a dip. She had a key employee leave and establish a competing business, taking a good portion of her business. She had two clients that went out of business while owing her $250,000 combined. What happened next is, again, an example of how fast life can change.

When she lost the major contract she downsized offices. She had $100,000 worth of leased office equipment that she no longer needed, nor could she afford. She let it go back, but the leasing company did not want it so she is in litigation over this. She also had a beautiful home in a gated community on the ocean, which has been foreclosed on. She is in litigation with the lender. She financed her receivables and so she continues to owe the $250,000 from the clients that went out of business. She is paying this back and it is having a horrendous effect on her cash flow. This woman who once would write a $5000 check for a mission through her church now doesn't have $5000 a month to live on. She, like my other friend, is depending on Social Security as her main source of revenue.

You might ask, didn't they plan? Of course they planned. No one wants to approach retirement and have all of their life's effort evaporate. Yet both of these people continue. They don't know how to throw in the towel. These reactions are internal. The two people I have just described are both great people with many accomplishments in their past. They are male and female. They are Republican and Democrat. They are from Florida and Michigan. When we look at the differences we can't help but see the similarities. These people are entrepreneurs who are not willing to give up regardless of the circumstances.

What keeps them going? I can only guess and draw from my experience. I believe it is pride, control, the desire to succeed, independence, and the need to make a contribution to society.

My Situation...

I'm going to spend a little time talking about my situation. In the early 1980's I was considered to be part of the American Dream. I owned my own successful business. I was married. I had two children, a cottage on one of the most beautiful lakes in Michigan, several boats, a nice home and money in the bank. Then my husband decided he wanted to leave a position with a major corporation and go into business for himself. I had reservations, but as part of a team (marriage) I supported the decision to leave the world of security and move into another family-owned business.

The business opened in July and in December our family fell apart. My husband left the business and the family. He left the debt behind and the economy was bad. Interest was high and the business was not making enough money to pay the bills. Everything we owned was leveraged against the loans for the business. I went through divorce and horrible business times. I worked that business along with the businesses I was already involved in and was mother to two children. It was a horrific time. I had youth on my side but my children suffered. They were 11 and 14 at the time and they worked in the business (restaurants) nights and weekends so we could have time together.

I worked days at my own businesses and the rest of the time at the restaurants. Interest was over 20%. It finally subsided and I sold the restaurants. I owed very large sums of money. The IRS came to my office and locked the doors. I filed for Chapter 11 reorganization and opened back up. I moved forward one step at a time.

I had a close friend help me write a letter to all my customers and employees to explain what was going on. I visited the local bankers and told them what was happening. Another friend with an advertising agency did TV spots. It happened to be the 12th anniversary of one of the companies, so I did an ad thanking our customers in the same dress I wore when the local news did top of the hour stories about the IRS locking the doors.

It worked. I hired the best local attorneys I could find. I trusted them and did what they told me. I came out of it. For years I paid monthly payments against the debt. During this time I came in contact with a consulting company that specialized in restructuring debt and workouts with the IRS and those without IRS obligations. I paid this company to assist me. It was so good to have someone dealing with all the issues that were out of my comfort zone. They saved me several hundred thousand dollars. I paid them, over time, approximately $50,000. I share the paying part because at the time I hesitated before engaging with the professionals. I thought that was a lot of money. It doesn't compare to the penalties and the interest, legal fees, accounting fees, overdraft bank charges and the embarrassment of levies on your account.

I learned a great deal going through this ordeal. I learned that the Federal Court House was not built solely for my use. There are lots of people who have gone before and after me. I learned that I was paying for the services I received and had a right to ask questions and expect what was best for me to happen. I learned it is okay to change accountants/lawyers if there is bad chemistry. I learned to listen and trust those I was paying for advice. I learned who my friends were and were not. I have often said it was like having a funeral without the need to die.

I moved forward one step at a time…

It was at that time I decided I would do what I could to help other people in the same or similar situation that I had experienced. I survived. My children grew up and got college educations. I met and married a great man. I devoted time to giving back and giving encouragement to people regardless of what issues they are facing.

Life is full of twists and turns and I found out that was not to be the end of my challenges.

When people ask me how is business, I am not sure what to tell them. In my reading and business education I have always been told to be in control and don't drone on about your problems. It makes customers and referral sources question your ability to do the job. So here is the problem. How is business? Fine? Horrible? My advice would be to figure out a response for several different questions regarding business. Some might be, "I'm continuing to learn and grow"; "Business could always be better but I am thankful for what I have in light of the economy"; "I'm just plugging along"' "I've got a few challenges right now, but that's business." You will have to pick your own.

That doesn't mean you can't seek the counsel of other business people. If my issue was insurance, I'd ask trusted peers if they had any experience in purchasing group health insurance, or worker's compensation or whatever it is. I would pick an issue, maybe finance-related, maybe legal. I'd ask one question and seek information from someone relating to one area. If you dump your entire bucket on someone they will back off rather than get too involved. You might need advice on something as simple or complex as pricing.

Don't forget to ask people to open doors for you. What do I mean? I mean make ask for introductions and/or tips on what a potential customer might be looking for or how decisions are made, or who the decision-maker is, or what their past experience is. When you start asking people to help you (network with you), be prepared to reciprocate.

Whatever your expertise is, be ready to advise. I know you probably don't feel like you have anything to share at this point. That is not true. You have much to share.

Write out your plan. I have used Mind Mapping as a successful tool. There are other tools that you could use. A list is better than nothing. The

Mind Mapping has helped me stay focused. It has helped me measure progress and it is so surprising to see the time elapse between the time you document and whatever day it is. Sometimes our path is interrupted; sometimes it takes longer than we hoped, but at least we keep our eyes on the path and have an end to focus on.

Is family involved in the business? When and what do you share with the family? This is different for each person. If you are single or if your problems don't involve family, you might keep everything close to your chest. If family is involved in the business, they must be informed of the situation. If you have family that has expertise in legal or accounting or business workouts, do you reach for their advice?

This is where emotion and pride come in. I, personally, elected to keep my problems to myself and look beyond family for guidance. I did this because of my pride. I also did this to protect my family. I didn't want to burden them with my issues. Was this right? I don't know. My immediate family includes several successful attorneys. I did end up going to them for legal advice and they were very upset with me for not coming to them sooner. This was one of the hardest things I have done. I can't speak for everyone but as a mother, wife, daughter, I have always viewed my role as one of helper and protector. Seeking help and answering questions and giving explanations of how the problems happened was not something I wanted to do, so I procrastinated. What I forgot was that the love and respect those around me have for me is not dependent on whether or not I am a success in business. It is based on who I am.

As I describe my issues with sharing, I must also tell you that my attitude and thought process have helped get me through the bad times. I have always thought about being successful, about the next projects, about helping others. I have never thought of curling up in a corner and throwing in the towel. If you think you can, as "The Little Train that Could", you can. If you think you can't, you probably won't.

22

Seek Help...

Numb. That is the word that best describes the feeling you get during the process of dealing with the financial problems you are facing. Numb is only one of the feelings you go through. You look at your desk and there are unopened and probably unanswered correspondence from whomever you owe money. The reason they are unopened or unanswered is part denial, part avoidance, but most importantly, there are no ready answers. What can you say to a creditor who wants to know when you plan on paying the outstanding balance? The choices: (a) make a promise you can't keep; (b) make a promise you might be able to keep; (c) tell them you don't have an answer; (d) ignore them; or (e) seek help. Obviously seeking help is the best solution.

That presents an entirely new set of problems and choices. What kind of help do I need? Who do I trust? How much will it cost? How will I pay for it? How can I continue to operate my business if I am spending all my time and resources with the help?

I will attempt to respond to the "seek help" options. This depends on many factors. It includes what you need, where you are located, who you have counted on in the past for advice and, most important, the trust and communication between you and the help. We can engage the best in the field, but if we can't understand them or if they can't understand us, we are wasting our resources and their time. The help has to be someone you can talk to, understand, and respect. This help is going to be your lifeline for the foreseeable future. What worked best for me was to identify a professional in one area and then use that professional to help me identify the rest of the team.

I'll give you an example. I used help in a situation where I was involved in a very large lawsuit with an insurance company. The lawsuit involved the agent, the insurance agency, the broker, and the insurance carrier. That is a lot of big city attorneys! My help person agreed with me that I needed an attorney. I decided I needed an attorney from a larger city than I was from. So in my case, I went to the Detroit market. How did I find the attorney? I contacted business friends from Detroit and asked for references. I selected an attorney and the suit got underway. Initially I paid a $5,000 retainer. We met and a plan was developed. Time passes, the clock ticks, and all parties involved except me have money to pay attorneys. One day I am over a year into this process and now in debt over $30,000 for legal fees. We have a meeting and I am told that I probably will not win this lawsuit. We look at my options. The options are not very appealing. My attorney first asks me to sign a personal agreement for his bill. Then he tells me I should talk with a bankruptcy attorney, start a new business and transfer my old business customers to the new business and put the new business in some other person's name. That is a lot to deal with.

He then invites a sage bankruptcy attorney to a meeting with me. I met this gentleman and I feel like I am watching a movie. The two attorneys tell each other how important they are and I sit by and watch. At the end of the conversation about how they have outwitted judges and juries, they refocus back on me. The bankruptcy attorney who has recently celebrated his 50th anniversary from University of Michigan Law School graduation tells me he will not be handling my case, his understudies will. He will do the courtroom obligations. He also tells me that he will need a retainer of $10,000 to research and see what our options are and how we should approach the legal issues. He tells me the total cost will be $50,000 or more. Somewhere in this meeting I tuned out. I could not comprehend this anymore.

I decided to seek a second opinion. I happen to have two very talented attorneys in my family. I purposely did not go to them prior to this point. I didn't want free help and knew they would not want to charge me. I also didn't want them to be concerned with my issues. Pride entered into the picture, too. Pride might have been the major contributor to my decision.

I secured new attorneys and we continued the fight. Throughout this process the business continues to operate. The day-to-day must continue. I also paid the first attorney. It was interesting because the first attorney offered a 10% discount if I paid the bill in full. I responded with I will pay monthly until paid in full, unless I am forced into filing bankruptcy, at which time the debt would become part of the bankruptcy. I share this story to explain how our attention and resources are subject to change at any time. One thing you can depend on is nothing today is the same as yesterday or the same as it will be tomorrow. Think of a roller coaster and hang on. Hopefully at the end of each ride there will be fear and triumph to remember.

This chapter started out with the word Numb. I got through many of the situations in a state of numbness. I am not strong enough to move through the path making the decisions and facing the issues that were necessary to get through. I know that many people face problems in their work place daily. Many people have lost jobs because their employers have gone out of business. I have not heard anyone from Delphi say, "I messed up so Delphi went out of business." In small business, the public looks at the situation and they don't say XYZ Company went out of business or had problems, they say Sharon Miller went out of business or had problems. The very reason entrepreneurs go into business is for the same recognition they achieve when they experience business problems. It is control.

The danger of "numb" is that it spills over into every facet of your life. You no longer have the ability to laugh from the belly, to embrace the many gifts life presents, to feel deeply. This is a dangerous place to be. It can have devastating effects on family, personal relationships, spiritual beliefs. I want to remind everyone that time does heal. We never forget some of the significant issues that we face during crisis, but time helps us deal with them. If we don't allow the situation to destroy, it strengthens. Keep strength in focus and know that one day in the future you will be stronger.

Let "numb" help you through some of the rough times, but don't let numb take control of your being today or in the future.

Financial Problems are a Financial Disease...

When I am talking with other business people it never fails that the question, "What's happening" comes up. The question usually is in reference to business, either mine or business in general, in the audience we both know. The information shared in these encounters is usually slanted, understated or overstated, depending on the storyteller.

So what happens when business owners finds themselves with financial problems? There will be people who point fingers and immediately blame the business owner, stating lack of talent, misuse of funds or some other negative reaction. There are those who look at the situation and say, "But for the grace of God, there I go."

Some people will distance themselves from you. They believe financial problems are a contagious disease. Financial problems are a financial disease. They just spread and get bigger and bigger until they are dealt with. Financial problems do not spread from one person to another, unless you loan money to other people. Many people are fearful that they will be asked to loan money and they would rather not get involved. I respect that position and tell people they should clearly state that position if/when they are asked to assist.

Friends and colleagues can assist with financial problems by making the person with the problems deal with the situation. Throwing money at the problem is not always the best fix. If your obligations are more than your cash flow, you must do something. Borrowing will only get you further in debt. Sometimes it means going lean. Sometimes it means facing business stoppage and moving to something better. If you are not making money, or in personal situations if your expenses are more than your income, things have to change. Why work for yourself if you go deeper in debt? Habit, pride, and other personal reasons. If you are facing personal financial problems, why live in a house you can barely make payments on while getting behind on taxes, insurance and utilities? Sometimes we focus on the wrong thing. The crisis we all face forces us to make the changes. We can look back and reflect on the emotion of the changes we make and usually will agree that life after the emotion of the change usually gets better.

In my life I went through a very difficult divorce. At the time I thought my life was never going to be normal again. I felt pain, hurt, despair and embarrassment. The feelings and the settlement of property and responsibilities stayed with me for a couple of years. Then one day I realized that the life I was living was much different. I had less, but I had peace, I had direction, I was happy. Each individual has to look at what they need in life versus what they think they need. There is a price to pay for happiness. The lack of financial independence makes life very difficult, but we each must evaluate and decide what financial independence really means. What is need and what is greed?

Make a Decision and Move Forward...

There is no beginning and no end. Each day you wake up and the world just spins. You are alone. You wonder if you should continue, run away, pray for life's end, or make some dramatic changes in your life. The changes are so hard to make. First, we must accept the position we are in. We feel defeated, but we should not feel defeated. Remember, many people are employees helping people like us that got in trouble with our businesses. Most people do not get in trouble because they are greedy. They get in trouble because they believe it will get better and wait too long before they make drastic changes.

One morning you get up and the world caves in on you. It might be real, it might be a mindset. Every human being has a point when enough is enough. Some people turn to drugs and alcohol. Some people run away from the problems (leave relationships, relocate). Some people ignore the problems and others stay to resolve the problems. Resolving problems will probably be the route most people go, but it is not going to be easy. It will be a real storm with the promise of new peace at the end.

These are the kinds of things you might be experiencing. Your bank account was levied. You are receiving certified mail from any number of people. There is probably legal action on a couple of fronts. Your building, home or auto needs repair. You are out of money and your ability to charge has vanished. This might be personal or it might be business or both. It is real. Your stomach aches, your head is splitting and you don't know what to do next.

Do you contact an attorney? A financial advisor? A friend? A workout specialist? It depends on your situation. The first thing you need to do is document everything you can think of regarding your situation. If you have a professional you trust and can communicate with, go there first. You will undoubtedly need advice from more than one of these professionals.

Once you start with a professional, keep journals on all of your calls and visits. You will be asked to complete a number of tasks, ranging from filling out financial information to assigning power of attorney. Each professional has their needs and their acronyms for forms, procedures and anything else they need.

My advice is to get a notebook and keep all reports, documents and correspondence by tabs in the notebook. It will relieve a great deal of stress.

Make copies of everything you give to one of these professionals. Don't be afraid to ask questions. You are paying for a service. Also ask for references, ask what the charges are and what they estimate the total charges are going to be. Ask about how long it will take. Keep asking questions, keep documenting. This process will save you time, money and frustration. It will also help the professionals you are working with. Tell all. You will think you have told all and then something else will pop up. Don't be afraid to dump your bucket. Open your mail. Act immediately and don't procrastinate. Nothing gets better by waiting when you are facing financial problems.

How are you going to pay for these services? Ask the professionals as you talk to them. Find out what you must pay. What comes first? Be prepared to change your entire outlook on life. There is no extra money at this time. It will be back to coupons, entertaining yourself without money, changing your buying, giving and dining habits. It will be back to the basics. At first that sounds very difficult, but in reality it really allows you to enjoy the things that are free.

This is also the time you have to face the future. Do you move? Close the business? Let someone else have the authority to operate and tell you what to do? Why did you and/or the business get into this mess? In my case, it was going for the gold and taking the risk for others. It was also the kind of business I was in. It was not about talent. This is a big hurdle to move around.

The most difficult part of facing financial problems and change is dealing with family and those you care about. You are embarrassed and don't want to disappoint others. I had to decide that my feelings for others are not centered around their financial status, so my worth and my wealth (or lack thereof) should not have an impact or bearing on my relationships.

When I woke up one Sunday morning and faced all of these things, I decided to move on to the next chapter in my life and do something about the situation I found myself in. I knew that if I didn't make a move I would continue to suffer emotionally and physically and something harmful would soon follow.

Say to yourself, "Today is the time to finish." Make a decision and move forward.

Tomorrow has Arrived...

The decision to face the problems, work through the crisis and plan for the future is now. It is a new place, a lot of new feelings surface. Feelings are in the body; reactions are in the head.

Where do I start? First I contact the professionals that I need. Do I need an attorney? A workout specialist? An accountant? That depends on where my problem lies and who I owe money to. Do I want to close the business? Sell the business? Work through the issues and continue to run the business? Is the business of value to anyone? If I walk away or close the business, what does that do to the debt? Will it follow me? Will it end and then I wait for years to reestablish myself? Do I lose everything? Will I have enough money to live? Where will I work?

I need to select professionals who I like and understand. Professionals who are straight forward and tell it like it is. (This is no time for making me feel good.) How am I going to pay for these professionals? How much will they cost?

First, I need to list all of my issues. Who I owe, for what, account numbers, date of debt, etc. A spreadsheet would be helpful. I need names, addresses, phone numbers and account numbers of all those I owe.

If I have real estate and lines of credit I probably need an accountant and attorney. If I have tax problems, I need a tax consultant and an attorney. I might need a business consultant, regardless of what my problems are. I need someone who can help me work through the layers that have been accumulating; someone without the emotional attachments that surround me.

I need to look at my overhead. If there are family members employed or on the payroll and not employed or if family members are overcompensated this will all change. If I have two new cars, charge cards and a six-figure salary, this will also change. I have to be ready to deal with reality. I don't, nor should I, give up hope. I should be thrilled that I have finally faced my challenges and life is about to change.

This is the time that I need to do research on tax consultants, business consultants and attorneys. Find out everything I can about them. When I call them I need to ask for references from clients that have been in the same situation as I have. That means similar business profile, similar age and similar financial situation. Then I need to follow through and check the references. Ask the questions. Did they do what they said? Were there surprises? Did it cost you a lot? How did you pay for it? Any question you might have should be asked. Hold these professionals to what they tell you. If you start with a professional and you can't communicate with them, find another one. Make sure you understand what they are saying and they understand what you are saying.

If you have to go to court during this process remember, the Courthouse was built before you entered the door. They do business there every day. You are not the only person to ever face these kinds of problems. Get through the day and then move forward. Look for peace in your life.

I had to take a look at how I did business, what business I did, what was profitable and what wasn't. I had to see if I had the right people on the bus, and if not, I needed to rearrange the seats or let some people get off the bus and let some new ones on the bus. I had to be open on how I was going to do business and reaffirm that it would never be the way it was before.

The Tax Man Cometh...

In my case it was the tax man and woman. I was at a point in business when every day I was trying to figure out how to pay the taxes owed. The money wasn't coming in as fast as the interest and penalties were accruing. Notices and intent letters came daily.

I decided to work from home one morning. I received a call from my office that I needed to come to the office immediately. I knew it was bad but couldn't know how bad.

Upon arrival I was greeted by the IRS representatives. They were closing me down. I didn't know what to do. I called a bankruptcy attorney and was fortunate enough to make contact. We talked about the mess I was in and what we could do. That day and the following week is still a blur.

When the IRS shuts you down, that is exactly what they do. They post a notice on the doors, change the locks, intercept the mail at both the building and the post office box, freeze the bank accounts, both business and personal, inventory and tag everything in the office, load any autos on flat bed trucks and take them away. They literally strip you of everything.

God gave me the ability to make decisions and I made the decision to keep fighting – move forward and don't retreat.

Where do you start? I contacted the attorneys. While I was doing that some employees were retrieving personal items and company records without the IRS seeing them. Other employees were crying, still others were praying. I had to meet with the attorneys. I had to notify employees, both those working in the office and those working on assignment for me at other locations. We moved the business to the house I was living in. I had just moved into a friend's house to sell it as they had moved out of state. The IRS didn't know where I was living.

I was blessed with core employees that hung in with me. They helped me contact clients and other employees, letting them know how to get in touch with us and what my plans were.

The attorneys went to court on Monday. We worked the weekend and they were able to get me opened back up for business on Monday morning. I went to the local banks and met with the bank presidents. I shared my story and the plans for the future. They worked with me and did not send payroll checks back. They allowed me time to get money in my account.

The date of this was one week before Christmas. There was little news and I had just been recognized by the Governor of Michigan the week prior to the seizure. I made the lead story for the local 6:00 and 11:00 p.m. news. Pictures of the building, interviews with an employee dropping off a timecard, and my photo from the Governor's recognition were all part of the story.

The very next morning I had a very prominent business person in town knock on my door and offered to purchase the business for pennies on the dollar. Other people called and offered support. No money, but support.

I financed my receivables at the time. I called the company I used and they were willing to continue providing financing for me.

The seizure happened on Friday and we went to court on Monday and were back in business. Naturally there were lots of questions from employees and clients and lots of decisions to be made.

I engaged a good law firm and I listened to what they said. They referred me to a business turnaround specialist who came in and pulled together the information needed for the courts. The turnaround specialist also took over running my business on a day-to-day basis. That was a real hard part. There were lots of questions asked a lot of different ways. I felt like the turnaround specialist was trying to trick me; like he didn't believe me. The truth, in retrospect, he was doing his job. He needed to know everything and it was obvious something had gone wrong. So with time and resistance some of my practices were changed to "best practices." We weren't doing things the best way. Our tracking and documentation were weak. We didn't have a real handle on the "cost of goods".

The internal workings of the business were changed. This led to a better business and documented proof of the ability to pay the IRS the monies due.

We also brought another specialist into the mix. We had our attorney (bankruptcy specialist), our turnaround specialist (operations), and the third one was a tax and debt consolidation specialist (someone to negotiate with the IRS on my tax liabilities). The tax experts review to make sure the records are correct; they work through all the forms and act as your liaison between the IRS and the person owing the debt. In addition we needed a good CPA firm and strong internal staff.

Everything comes with a price. I remember wondering where the money would come from. Determination and faith helped me move forward on a daily basis. We got beyond that horrible day in December.

I have told many about the funny things and the humbling things that transpired during this time frame. A friend came over with lovely Christmas gifts for my daughters and me. Two members from my Zonta Club brought cookies and came for a visit. One of the members offered me money to finish my Christmas shopping. A business acquaintance from Flint came to my office and did a commercial celebrating 12 years in business for one of my businesses. I wore the same dress that I wore when I received the Governor's Award. This was the clip they aired as a lead-in to the news.

The letters I mailed to employees and clients were done on the weekend. The letter was drafted by a friend. I had employees who furnished food, offered support and prayer. I had one young employee who offered to work for free.

My bookkeeper, a man probably at retirement age, went home and never came back. I have no idea what happened to him.

I received letters and notes of encouragement from people I worked with in the past. I've told many it was like a funeral without dying. The process created a newfound realization of how good people are.

My family, my daughters in particular, were always supportive and willing to help. With the help of good professionals and good friends, we moved forward.

Bankruptcy…

Businesses often fail to plan prior to bankruptcy. Filing a bankruptcy usually only delays the inevitable. Failure to plan usually leads businesses filing for bankruptcy to failure and a waste of money.

One of the Bankruptcy Exchange founders, John O'Neill, has a favorite saying. "If you go to a candy store, you are going to get candy." What he is really saying is, "If you go to a bankruptcy attorney, you are most likely going to file bankruptcy." Huge fees to the attorney and the court can follow.

Having said that, let it be known there is a great need for good bankruptcy attorneys. These are the attorneys who do the planning and take proper action ahead of time. There are attorneys who do not have the business background to do consulting and don't know how to run a business. They understand the academic part of running a business but don't understand the applied part. They don't know how to make cuts. The longer you stay in bankruptcy, the longer the attorney gets paid.

Attorneys are not getting paid to correct the problems. If you file for bankruptcy without addressing the problems, you will have a repeat of the same stressful business situation again. When a consultant reviews the petition, they examine them based on industries they know how to run. Good consultants deal with businesses with which they feel they can make a difference.

When a business faces the IRS, there is often the perception that a deal can be brokered where pennies on a dollar are paid and everything will be fine. Don't heed the advertisements that make you believe "one fix to all problems." This is the wrong way to approach a troubled business.

Tomorrow...

The most important thing tomorrow can bring is peace of mind. Living in the present. We can't have peace of mind when we are preoccupied with past mistakes and failures. We need to stay involved in whatever we are interested in. Keep friends and family close. Revel in the now. Peace of mind can't be purchased, yet it is within reach of all of us. Doing something about our problems and developing a new plan allows us to start the journey to peace of mind.

Recommendation:

Bankruptcy Exchange is a company that provides services to businesses and individuals facing bankruptcy. Bankruptcy Exchange operates proactively. Review of Chapter 11 bankruptcies is done daily. Companies that meet the criteria our company specializes in are identified.

Bankruptcy Exchange has consulting teams with a wide range of expertise and have turned around many small businesses.

Bankruptcy Exchange embraces companies that have IRS debt. The IRS will control how the bankruptcy is administered. Bankruptcy Exchange works with the IRS on buy-out options. In this type of transaction, the IRS is usually the first paid, and many times the only creditor paid. Secured creditors are paid if there are assets or funds. Other creditors will not receive payment.